RETIRE
AND GROW RICHER!

*The Continuing Saga of One Man's
Quest to Save his Retirement
from the Great Recession, Divorce,
and the Mexican Drug Wars!*

Marcus Arce
Meme Media

Retire and Grow Richer!™
Published by Meme Media.

ISBN-13: 978-1490969381
ISBN-10: 1490969381
Copyright © 2013 by Marcus Arce.
All rights reserved.

Printed in the United States of America.

10 9 8 7 6 5 4 3 2 1

I dedicate this second part of my
unfolding drama to all the kids…
my nieces and nephews and their kids, too!

Our crazy, cool extended family…
dream big and reach far!

I love you all.

PREFACE

In my book, *Retire and Grow Rich!*, I tell of how I saved my retirement by investing a big chunk of my retirement savings in rental properties. And, by a *big chunk*, I mean much, much more than any sane financial advisor would consider prudent—almost $200,000 of the $300,000 I had left after my divorce in August of 2012.

My primary goal in doing that, investing in those rental properties, I mean, was to replace the monthly income I was paying to my ex as part of the divorce settlement and cover the monthly cost of my own housing, as well. If I could achieve those two goals, I figured I could afford to stay retired.

If not, then, I would either have to curtail my lifestyle dramatically or give up being retired and be forced to find a job; both being options no retired person ever wants to face!

The bottom-line for my little real estate enterprise was actually to net $2,000 a month from rents and imputed income. And, as it turned out, I was able to start generating that much income, and then some, just sixty days from the day I closed escrow on my first rental property in late 2012.

Using a large part of what I had left of my retirement savings, I paid cash for that first property: $85,000.

Subsequent to that purchase, I entered into a contract to purchase a second rental property. This was only days after going into escrow for the first and both properties were in escrow at the same time. I also used my retirement savings to pay cash for that property: $95,000

The first property, what I call my *Ranchita*, consists of four individual rental *units*: One of the units is an 1,800 square foot house with three bedrooms, two full bathrooms, and a large eat-in kitchen.

Also situated on the two acre, fenced lot is a smaller *casita*, and two trailer homes. The property is zoned for horses and includes three stalls and an entirely fenced, one-quarter acre pasture.

The property sits a stone's throw from the banks of the Colorado River!

That second property was two separate houses on single lot. The lot was almost one full acre and it was zoned commercial. The lot, alone, was (and is) worth more than what I paid for it at the time I purchased it.

But generating more income was only the first part of the plan—and how I accomplished that goal is what I detail in my first book.

The second part of the plan was to grow my net worth and replace the $300,000 I had lost in the time between when my (now) ex-wife and I separated and the day the final decree was signed-off on by the judge.

I did mention that second part of my plan in my first book, but did not go into depth on how I planned to accomplish that goal. In this book, I finish the story.

The plan in this book, like the plan in my first book, might just be your ticket to a better retirement lifestyle—it certainly proved to be so for me!

In my first book, I tell about how, after being comfortably retired for five years, and married for almost ten, my wife and I separated and the divorced.

In that book, I also relate the financial cost of that separation and divorce. How much?

Well, by the time it was all said and done, I lost just about one-half of my retirement savings, a loss of almost $300,000, and almost twenty percent of my monthly, net pension income by way of the monthly support payments I am obligated to provide her (my ex-wife) until 2017.

This, then, is the second part of the story.

Table of Contents

INTRODUCTION

I mentioned that it was the financial loss I suffered in my divorce that made it necessary to begin investing in rental properties again after cashing out of the business a few years before. But what you should also know is that, on the day the divorce was final, I was sixty years old.

At that age, I did not have the luxury of wasting time by feeling sorry for myself, although I have to admit that I did waste some doing just that.

You see, it is one thing to be in the position of needing to start over at 30, I know because I had been in that position, as well, but it is another thing entirely to be in that position at sixty!

There I was, alone again, after fifteen years with the same woman. I still remember feeling the weight of the world on my shoulders for the first few months after our divorce was final.

At the time I retired, after a thirty-year career with the United State Federal Government, I started receiving an annual pension of just about $50,000 a year based on those thirty years of government service and I also had approximately $600,000 cash in savings.

Not bad, I know, but then it all started going south…literally!

In the time between the day I retired and the day the divorce was final, I lost, as I said, about one-half of my retirement nest-egg—a loss of almost $300,000!—and almost twenty percent of my pension to her in the way of monthly support payments.

And, by the terms of our settlement, she also got to remain living in the house we had previously shared. Suddenly I found myself without a place to call home for the first time in a very long time and living alone in a cramped hotel room.

As you might imagine, my mood at the time was not great!

After only a couple of weeks in that hotel, however, a friend had a small rental house he owned come available and, eager for more space, I moved into it. That house was on the south side of the Mexico/USA border, just a few miles from Yuma, Arizona, the small city I had been living in at the time of my divorce.

Alone, lonely, and hiding from the world in that tiny house in that small Mexican border town, I spent way too much time sitting in the dark, drinking and licking my wounds….feeling sorry for myself, mostly.

Confused by my feelings of regret, loss, and loneliness, for some reason I fixated on the money; all I could think about, it seemed, was all the money that was gone, seemingly vanished into thin air, and the money that I was now bleeding every month in the form of those support payments to my ex-wife.

I became somewhat obsessed with the question of how I could possibly recover all that had been lost—and I do not mean just the money:

I was thinking about all the years lost to the relationship that was now just so much, still hot ash and the years that had seemingly flown by only to arrive at a place I had never calculated into all my prior, careful retirement planning.

But, in addition to the relationship issues, the financial reality of my post-divorce situation was certainly a big reason for the funk into which I had descended by that time! Had I really blown it, I wondered, to the extent that I would now, at my age, need to start pounding the pavement again to find a job?

My biggest concern was that what I had left, of all I had once had, would now not be enough to finance my retirement for the next…well, for however long I might live?

That was a dangerous question for a man with a bottle, a bad attitude, and too much time alone on his hands.

It was another night like so many of the recent past—a beer in hand, a bottle of tequila, a shot glass, and the lights off—that I made the decision to get off my ass and get on with my life.

It had been a good run, I thought to myself, but that run was over. I can sit here until my liver gives out, my self-talk continued, or I can start another run. I decided to start another run!

And I knew of only one opportunity that I could take advantage of that would not only afford me the chance to recoup my losses and save my retirement but get me re-engaged with the world from which I had been slipping away for the past few months.

That opportunity? Owning rental houses.

PART ONE

Growing Wealth In
Retirement With Real Estate

CHAPTER ONE

I had had some measured success in the rental property business in the past; and in the not too distant past I had made just about $250,000 buying, selling and owning real estate. In the more distant past, I had made roughly $100,000 buying and selling a few properties in the eighties.

Real estate had been the source, both directly and indirectly, of much of my $600,000 nest egg.

But, by the time I divorced, I had been largely out of the business for a few years, except that, like many other homeowners at the time, I found myself something of an accidental landlord as a result of the Great Recession.

The property to which I am referring was geographically inconvenient to keep and expensive to maintain. It was a 5,000 square foot, two story house with four bedrooms and three bathrooms located on a large, ocean-view lot in a gringo enclave in Baja California Norte, Mexico.

My (ex) wife and I had purchased it as a vacation home in better times; late-2007 to be exact. By the time of our divorce, it was something of an albatross around my neck and as hammered as real estate in the USA had been the last few years (2008 to 2011), you can imagine what the market was like in Mexico.

Gringos wanting to relocate to the drug-wars down south were few and far between!

Luckily, I managed to sell it just before I decided to get back into the rental business, regardless. The thing is, I sold it for a lot less than it had cost me and that loss was part of the total of the losses that I suffered during that time.

I knew that my best chance of recouping those losses was by getting back into the rental property business and, that by doing so, I could also cure the lethargy I was feeling at the time, as well.

You see, I love houses. I love looking for houses to buy, walking through their empty rooms, inspecting them to uncover their faults and hidden charms, and owning them. I get excited by the potential of a vacant house to become the sacred space of a home. Real estate, I knew, could reenergize me!

And, as I have mentioned, I had made some money in real estate in the past and felt confident I could do it again: I knew the recipe…

The divorce had taken the wind out of my sails but I knew that there was a good chance that the process of acquiring a rental property or two and then managing those properties, myself, might just fill that cloth once more.

And I had something to prove to myself, as well! I wanted to prove that the divorce was not going to mark the end of the good life but, rather, just the point at which I had transitioned to what came next— an even better life! I needed, I knew, to get back into the business so that I might begin to live again.

I had two goals: Rebuild my net monthly income to what it had been before the divorce and continue to grow my net worth in an effort to replace those savings I had lost in the past twenty-four months.

The next morning, I went for a run for the first time in something like five months.

When I got back from the run, I showered and shaved, and sat down to develop a five year plan to accomplish those two goals by investing the retirement savings I had left in rental real estate.

I did not want to simply survive the divorce, I wanted to thrive. As I have already mentioned, my first book tells how I accomplished my first goal—more monthly income through the vehicle of only a couple of rental property investments.

In this book, you will learn how I accomplished my second goal—grow my net worth by the $250,000 in just thirty-six months.

And, for those of you who have not yet read *Retire and Grow Rich!*, I have included a preview of it at Appendix One of this book.

CHAPTER TWO

Divorce has only one cause—marriage! And I do not say that to be trite or in an attempt at gallows humor.

I will never get married again because I never want to give people I do not know, do not care for, and whom I would never associate with if not forced to do so, access into my life, and control over it, ever—NEVER!—again.

Fool me once, shame on you. Fool me twice…ain't gonna happen!

And, I am happy to report that, at this point in the unfolding story that is a life, I have moved on and well on my way, now that I have achieved my first goal of more monthly income, to achieving my second goal of growing my net worth by $250,000 in the next three years.

Ambitious, I know, especially when you consider that that represents an increase of almost 100%. And, so, I am sure you must be wondering, how exactly did I plan to achieve that goal?

Two ways:

1. Acquire approximately $400,000 worth of real estate and let appreciation work its magic, and;

2. Savings from income.

In the six months after buying my first rental property, my net worth has grown, I would estimate, by approximately $100,000.

$75,000 of that amount was from the instant equity I realized on two of the properties I purchased during that time for less than market value, the rest of it from appreciation on my properties, tax savings, and monthly income above my monthly cost of living.

So, and in other words, not too long after the day my divorce was final, I had recouped almost one-half of the money I had lost!

And, at the same time that I was in the process of acquiring the two properties, I was also paring down my living expenses. When the rental income started coming in, I had reduced my monthly cost of living to less than $3,000 and that figure includes the $700 I pay my ex every month.

Today, as I write this, my gross annual income is over $80,000 and I am banking more than $3,000 a month. Barring any unexpected expenses, my income, alone, will grow my net worth by almost $40,000 a year from now on!

And I fully expect that, by the end of the twelve months since my first rental property purchase in December of 2012, to have grown my net worth by a total of $150,000, or close to that, anyway!

And consider this, if you will: that $150,000 annual figure is way more than I ever back when I was working for a living!

This coming year, 2014, I will, I expect, gross less than that because I won't have the benefit of the instant equity realized in 2013; $100,000 is my guess.

These figures include the income from my pension, writing, and rents and the appreciation on all my real estate, as well.

As I write this, I look out the window of my beach house in a small resort town in Baja California Norte, Mexico. I can see dolphins skimming across the surface of the ocean.

It is almost Happy Hour in our little seaside hacienda in paradise…I call out to my new amiga to bring me a beer. It has been another grueling four-hour work day, pounding away at the keyboard…oh…and my property manager called to say she had deposited the rent checks!

My real estate investments are what provide me this life. I am earning something like ten thousand dollars a month and spend less than three of those thousands to support my lifestyle.

And, again, $700 of my monthly nut is support I pay my ex-wife.

I remember wondering, when I first got divorced, if paying her that money every month—losing, if you will, that big a chunk of my retirement income— would mean I would have to come out of retirement and go back to work. These days, however, I don't give those payments to her a thought and, in a couple of years they end, regardless.

I can't believe that I once lost sleep over that money…but, believe me, I did!

Thankfully, I have more than enough and I hope the money I give her every month helps her. I really do…really…I do…And, when my obligation to provide her those support payments ends, it will mean almost nothing to me—just that much more to my savings every month.

But, when all is said and done and written, this is not a book about money, not really. This is a book about creating a new life after a two-year stretch in hell.

The divorce was two years of lawyers, and judges and harsh words; two long, long years of sleepless nights, too much booze, and fear and loathing. And our divorce was fairly amicable…I think…I have only been through the one but I have heard some real horror stories in this regard. Our divorce was never all that hostile.

CHAPTER THREE

Still, my divorce was no picnic. And the events were made even worse by the fact that I am a sensitive guy prone to self-doubt and much inward contemplation; too much, really.

During the divorce I lost almost forty pounds to the stress of it. I read somewhere that a divorce reduces a man's life by seven years and, based on my own personal experience, I can believe it!

I cannot afford to lose another forty pounds, that's for sure! Which means that, if you do the math, I simply would not survive another divorce. To marry again could prove to be an act of suicide on my part.

But, then, when the divorce was final and the lawyers and judges were gone from my life, and the intrusiveness of the whole process was over almost as suddenly as it had all began, I just as suddenly realized I was free!

I WAS FREE!

And now I could, at last, move on to what was next.

Although, at the time, I had no idea what next was going to be, exactly. I was simply too exhausted to even think about it at the time.

My first book is about what did come next; this book is about what came after what came next.

CHAPTER FOUR

My divorce did have one positive aspect to it— fortuitous timing.

When my divorce became final, the local real estate market, after years of staggering losses, was beginning to show signs of life. House prices were still way down from their previous highs and good deals were still available but there was a light at the end of a four year tunnel that was the national financial crisis that almost took us all down.

In fact, by some accounts, house prices in Yuma were up over fifteen percent in the past twelve months!

This, then, was the market into which I stepped, determined to rebuild my net worth and grow my monthly income. And I had three-hundred thousand dollars with which to finance the rebuilding of my life. I could not have asked for a better opportunity, frankly.

As I have previously detailed, I paid cash for the two investment properties I purchased; investing the biggest part of my retirement savings to do so. You might be wondering why I did, in fact, pay cash—particularly if you already understand the financial implications of paying cash vice getting a mortgage.

And the reason I paid cash is not because I would not have qualified for a mortgage.

No, the reason I paid cash is because it was the most efficient way to meet my goal of an additional $2,000 of NET monthly income.

By paying cash, all the rental income above operating costs is mine as monthly income. If I had financed those purchases, I would have had two mortgages to pay.

And a mortgage is expensive! In fact, in the first five years of a typical, market-rate mortgage…let's use 6% as an example…something like ninety-five cents of every dollar you pay, on average, over those five years, is interest.

By avoiding a mortgage, I also avoided that cost! And the money that would have gone to the bank, as interest, went into my own pocket to support my lifestyle, instead.

Paying cash maximized my cash-flow on each of the properties, if not my return on investment (ROI).

And, in this instance, it was cash I was after although the ROI I was realizing from rents and imputed income, alone, was orders of magnitude greater than what the money had been earning me in the bank.

Now, I could have achieved the same result, in terms of monthly rental income, by financing several properties. However, by paying cash, I only had to buy two properties to meet my income goal AND more properties would have meant that much more work—my primary goal was not more work, it was more monthly income!

The goal to grow my net worth was secondary to my more immediate need to generate more income and thereby be able to afford to remain retired. And, once all the elements of my plan were in place, I knew that my net worth would grow of its own accord.

And, besides, as I alluded to previously, the savings that I used to pay cash for those two properties was basically wasting away in the bank. I was earning a measly .003% interest on it—less than $50 a month. I simply needed the money I had left (after my divorce) to work harder than that!

CHAPTER FIVE

How do you measure success? How do you know, at the end of the day, month, or year, whether or not it has been a good day (month or year) or not? There is only one way, really, and that is to measure your progress towards your goals.

In my first book, I wrote about a period of time when my savings grew by leaps and bounds. This was when I was living in one of the units of two-unit building (a duplex; two individual but connected, usually by a common wall, housing units; apartments, if you will). The other unit was rented and the monthly rent covered the mortgage payment and, most months, even the utility bills.

What you need to be aware of is that, in a situation like that, you are receiving, what is known as, imputed income; that is, I was living rent-free in the half of the duplex I was occupying as my primary residence. But, *and this is important*, because I was not paying rent, I was able to allocate the money that would have been going to pay my cost of housing to other uses.

I was actually benefitting from two separate streams of income—the imputed income of rent I didn't pay and the growth in my net worth when I banked the money I would otherwise have been spending to pay the mortgage.

I ended up saving an additional $1,000 a month— $12,000 a year and PLUS I was living rent-free.

Anyone, including you, can do the same thing but most people choose a single-family residence to provide for their housing needs. That is the almost always more expensive than the arrangement I describe.

Rent-free living, on the other hand, boosts your NET income.

When you pay cash for a property, and live in one of the units, yourself, the financial dynamic is slightly different. In that case, the rent you receive PLUS the value of the imputed income equals your gross ROI. Again, a specific example from my own investments:

One of my properties, let's call it the Palm House, is two separate houses on one lot:

NOTE: This is not a duplex; a duplex is two connected units.

I rented the smaller house for $550 a month and lived in the other, larger house, myself. The house I live in, I could rent for approximately $900 a month.

And what all those numbers add up to is $1,450 a month of cash and imputed income.

I purchased the property for $95,000 cash and spent another $5,000 on various repairs and improvements to get the one house ready to rent and the other ready for me to live in.

Again, my gross monthly income on the property, counting only the rent and imputed income, was $1,450.

Based on just those two streams of income, my gross ROI was as follows:

(1450) (12)/(100,000).

Doing the math, then, it comes to 17.4%.

17.4%!

Remember, that same money, in the bank, had been earning me a very measly .003%...a just as measly twenty-five bucks a month!

And, really, I was losing money on that money when it was sitting in the bank because the rate of inflation was higher than the interest rate I was earning at the time.

Obviously, operating expenses will lower that ROI figure, but other considerations, such as tax savings, act to boost it right back up again.

And, it is likely that the gross ROI will continue to climb over time as rents increase and because, I believe, the rate of appreciation is going to increase, for the next few years, at least!

By the way, I rented the one unit for slightly under the market rate—$550. I did so for a couple of reasons. One, the tenant paid all the utility bills and maintained the lot and landscaping. The second reason is that I wanted the rent to be a good deal in order to entice the tenants to stay there a long time.

In some rental-property management books, they will tell you that if tenants are not moving out every couple of years or so, it is likely that it is because your rents are too low. On the other hand, nothing kills rental profits like a vacancy, and I do raise rents every year…that annual increase is written right into the rental agreement.

But the most work in this business is preparing a property to rent, screening potential tenants, and getting them moved in. I like to avoid that work and I am willing to pay for doing so; that "paying" I do by giving my tenants a good deal. And, again, if one of your rentals stays vacant for a month or two (or longer!), your annualized ROI is going into the tank and you are losing money!

But all that is just by way of explaining my own preferences and property-management style. Your mileage may differ, as they say!

PART TWO

Money In The Bank

CHAPTER SIX

There is a big difference between money in the bank and money in a rental property—let me explain:

First, let me say that money in the bank, that is, money in any account where the principle is guaranteed would seem to be a sure-thing and without risk...except it is not, not really. If the interest the account is paying you is less than the rate of inflation in the general economy, then the buying power of your money is going down.

In other words, you are losing money even though the principle (the money you actually deposited, yourself) is guaranteed. So, even though you might think that money in such an account is risk-free, that is simply not the case if the interest rate is less than the inflation rate.

But there is risk of that nature and, then, there is risk of the nature you will assume when you own rental properties.

The right kind of insurance can act to greatly mitigate the risk of personal liability such as some oversight or failure to perform on your part that causes injury to the tenant or someone else on your property.

Then there is the risk to the capital you have invested in the property. This risk is greatest on a mortgaged property when the owner is under-financed; that is, if the owner does not have the capital reserves (i.e.; money in the bank) to "carry" the property when it is not rented for any reason.

When you pay cash for a property, there is no risk of losing the property to foreclosure but fail to pay your property taxes long enough and you could lose your property to the county.

But risks aside, I want to compare money in the bank to the income from a rental property when one is living off the principle:

In the financial realm, there resides a mythical beast known as the "safe-withdrawal" rate (SWR). This is the rate at which you can, theoretically, safely withdraw money from a cash account to pay living expenses without depleting the principle, itself.

The safe-withdrawal rate is generally assumed by financial planner-types, when they do their financial-planning thing, to be in the three to six percent range; that is, their calculations are based on the assumption that the account will earn an average annual interest-rate that will fall somewhere in that range. This figure is based on a mix of historical data such as stock-market returns and the interest rate on bonds.

But guess what? In the past few years, as I write this in late-2013, that assumption has long since gone out the window. Stocks tanked and the average of interest rates paid on savings have been at an all-time low...and they have been there for a long time now!

In that sort of financial environment, there is no such a thing as a safe withdrawal rate!

On the one hand, financial advisors will give you an assumed rate and use it to determine your SWR during retirement, and on the other hand, they will tell you that past performance is no guarantee of future returns.

In other words, they are blowing smoke to a very large extent and at your possible expense!

Anyway, bottom-line, what they are telling you is that you can withdraw any earnings to spend as income.

That assumption, however, is based entirely on the assumption that interest rates and returns going forward will be in line with those historical, long-range averages.

That assumption, however, has something of a fatal flaw. And that flaw has been exposed in the last few years when the government intervened to first depress interest rates and then keep them artificially low for years while, at the same time, the stock market, as I mentioned, tanked.

During that time, a whole lot of people lost a whole lot of money and many retired folks found themselves needing to get themselves un-retired real quick!

As I write this in mid-2013, those retirement savings I keep in insured, guaranteed accounts are earning me less than one-half of one-percent a year!

And my earnings have been in that range for a couple of years now!

CHAPTER SEVEN

Anyway, back to the assumption of a safe withdrawal rate…

Based on that assumption, a financial planner will tell you that x amount of dollars will earn x amount of income and the income your savings earn you can skim off the top without depleting the principle and you never have to worry about running out of money.

Sounds good, right? Right. Except for one thing— there is no such thing as a safe-withdrawal rate based on some historical average regardless of its provenance:

You can only safely withdraw what your retirement savings account has actually earned in the past year less expenses; and even that only applies if the interest rate you are earning is greater than the inflation rate.

Let me repeat that last little bit of bad news:

You can only safely withdraw what the account earned in the past year less expenses; and even that only applies if the interest rate you are earning is greater than the inflation rate.

In other words: You can only safely withdraw those earning that are above inflation.

If your average ROI is 4% and inflation is 3%, then you can only safely withdraw 1%. Unless you have a HUGE amount of savings, one percent won't frost the cake or gild the lily!

And, unless you follow that rule, you are spending principle and, so, you are also, effectively, losing money and the future buying-power of your money is diminishing. Diminish it enough and guess what? You are broke!

AGAIN: As I write this in June of 2013, my retirement savings in guaranteed, short-term accounts is earning about .003%...less than one-half on one percent, in other words. And, even though it looks as if I am earning something, as little as that might be, because the inflation rate is more than what I am earning, I am—ABSOLUTELY—losing money!

For the past five years, as I have written, the Federal government has kept interest rates artificially low and anyone who assumed they would earn the historical average when they retired is probably pounding the pavement in search of a job by now!

But by investing my retirement savings in rental properties, I am now earning several times what that same amount of money had been earning me sitting safely in the bank!

How much more?

Well, let's look at the actual numbers of my Palm House one more time:

Again, I purchased the property for $95,000 cash and spent another $5,000 on various repairs and improvements to get the one house ready to rent and the other ready for me to live in. My gross monthly income on the property, counting only the rent and imputed income, was $1,450.

Based on just those two streams of income, my ROI was (1450) (12)/(100,000).

Doing the math, then, it comes to 17.4%. Obviously, operating expenses will lower that figure, but other considerations, such as tax savings, act to boost it right back up.

So how many times greater is my return on that particular property than what I earn on my safe money in the bank? Let's do the math:

17.4/.003 = 5,800

Unbelievable, right?

But the numbers don't lie.

CHAPTER EIGHT

But that is not the point I want to make or what I actually want to bring to your attention. And that is this:

If you are living off your saving you might be unlucky enough to live so long as to out-live your savings and run out of money.

That is a sort of worst-case scenario for us retired types!

But that can never happen if I am living off rental income. Remember, I have no mortgage payment— the rents I receive are mine to keep. Some of that money goes to pay expenses related to the property, itself, but the rest is mine to spend in support of my monthly costs of living if I so choose or need to use it that way.

Spending that money does nothing to undermine the value of the property; taking money out of a rental property in the form of rental income does not lower your net worth like spending your savings does.

In fact, during periods of normal inflation and appreciation in the housing market, my net worth is growing…day by day, month by month, and year after year.

And, what I knew going into the implementation of my investment strategy, and what I counted on, as well, was that appreciation in housing prices would be how I would achieve my goal to grow my NET WORTH.

And that appreciation is tax-free until I sell, if ever! It is something like a 401k in this regard except that I don't fund it every year out of my own pocket—my tenants do that for me!

At the time I started buying real estate again in 2012, all the signs pointed to a recovery in the real estate market. I fully expected house prices to climb an average of 15% a year for the next three years. How did I come up with that 15% figure? That is how long it would take home builders to get going again and supply the housing supply necessary to meet the demand.

You see, when the housing bubble exploded, credit got tight, and housing demand almost vanished overnight! People stopped buying and builders stopped building—in fact, some builders even abandoned half-built houses—they simply instructed the carpenters and other workers to pack up an never come back.

When demand went down, prices followed. Now, as the housing market improves, buyers who are looking to purchase a personal residence, but had been waiting for the dust to settle, are back in the market— these are fueling much of the rise in house prices— but not all of it!

Add to that demand the fact that banks have sold off the majority of their inventory of foreclosures. Many of them to private parties but institutional investors are snapping them up in large lots, as well, because they see what's happening!

Also, short-sales are largely becoming a thing of the past since housing prices have started to jump. And, there being almost no new houses available, we are fast approaching a scenario not unlike the feeding frenzy that preceded the bubble popping!

I have a few friends that are real estate agents and they say they have NEVER been busier or closing more deals. The only reason they are not even busier, they tell me, is that the supply of houses is so low.

In fact, according to the Associated Press, Phoenix, Arizona, one of the cities hit hardest by the collapse in real estate prices, saw prices increase by something like 25% in the twelve months between March of 2012 and March of 2013.

Knowing all that, and knowing what those signs are pointing to, I established the goal of owning $400,000 worth of real estate.

And how did I arrive at that $400,000 figure as my goal? Well, it was something of a balancing act, actually.

I am in a financial position now that I could buy another property once or even twice a year. But, as of today, I won't do so because each additional property would mean that much more risk and work for me. I feel like I have as much of either as I want or need to assume at this point in my life and as much as I need to meet my goals.

And, again, my two goals were to continue growing my net worth while, at the same time, using some of the income from the rental properties to pay my costs of living while also off-setting the amount I am paying my ex per the terms of our divorce settlement.

Again, in the twelve months between March of 2012 and March of 2013, Phoenix house prices surged 22.4%. 22.4/12 = 1.8% per month appreciation. I, however, live in Yuma, Arizona and this is where I own my real estate, as well.

Yuma did not do as well as Phoenix. Yuma house prices, according to an article on CNNMoney.com, last updated in May of 2012, were expected to rise 16.7% in the following twelve months. I read this back in late 2012, about the time I started amassing my $400,000 in real estate, and I assumed a more modest 15% average increase for the next three years for planning purposes.

CHAPTER NINE

Let me now further explain some of what I touched on in that last chapter, but in another way; in a way that I, personally, like to think of as the shape-shifting of capital:

In real estate, there is a concept known as, *highest and best use.*

Wikipedia describes the concept as follows:

Highest and best use, or highest or best use (HBU), is a concept in real estate appraisal that shows how the highest value for a property is arrived at.

When you seek to establish the market value of real property, that value must be based on its highest and best use.

Highest and best use is always that use that would produce the highest value for a property, regardless of its actual current use.

The Appraisal Institute of Canada defines the concept as follows:

HIGHEST AND BEST USE: the reasonably probable and legal use of property, that is physically possible, appropriately supported, and financially feasible, and that results in the highest value.

Any proposed or theoretical use of a property must pass a series of tests before it can be accepted as the highest and best use of the property. In some cases, a proposed use might be the highest and best use but for some cost that changes the net economics.

An example might be an industrially-used site that can now be used legally for high-rise residential buildings, but would cost so much to clean up (remediate) that the value as currently used is higher. In that case, if it can be continued, the existing industrial use could be the highest and best use.

Well, guess what? The same concept can be applied to the cash that represents your retirement savings. In order to understand how it does apply, we need to look at a net worth statement:

When you have $100,000 in the bank and you withdraw $5,000 to cover living expenses, your balance is then $95,000.

But, when you use that $100,000 to purchase a rental property, your net worth is the same, only the form of that value has now changed.

CHAPTER TEN

Cash is the single, most liquid form of capital. When you take cash and turn it into something other than cash, like when you use it to purchase real estate, the bottom-line on your net worth statement *might* still be the same, but it is no longer as liquid as it was when it was cash.

In order to make the value in that asset liquid again, you would first need to convert it back to cash. In the case of a pressing need for cash, this conversion process could be a problem.

There is a term: *house rich, cash poor.*

It describes a financial state that is exactly what we are discussing here: Equity but no cash.

And cash has no real responsibility attached to it; you do not need to keep cash painted or rented or otherwise maintain cash. A rental property does require work to maintain the value originally stored in it.

A rental property also has some risk attached to it; considerably more risk than cash, although cash does present some risk since it can lose value even when stored in an account where the principle is *guaranteed.*

The fact that equity is not as liquid as cash is one reason why I did not invest all of the savings I had left after my divorce in real estate. Instead, I kept $100,000 in cash as operating capital. Businesses often fail for lack of operating capital and owning rental real estate is a business, after all.

But back to my point, spending any principle amount of your savings will reduce the balance of your savings. In order to preserve your principle, you can only spend the amount you actually earned on your savings that is above inflation.

Remember: When my $300,000 was sitting in the bank, for most of the time between 2009 and 2012, I was earning less than one-half of one percent on those savings. And, because the rate of inflation was greater than that amount, I was actually losing money!

And what that meant is that I could not withdraw any money from my savings because to do so would have meant that I was spending principle: Do that and you run the possibility of out-living your money!

But when I converted $190,000 of my retirement savings into rental real estate, I lost liquidity and gained risk, but gained income and protection from inflation. My net worth statement was virtually unchanged but my income statement improved dramatically!

And whereas spending the principle of your savings will reduce the balance and, so, your net worth by the same amount of however much you do spend, spending rental income, even if you spend all of it, does not reduce your net worth.

CHAPTER ELEVEN

In fact, in an appreciating real estate market, your net worth will still grow—even if you are spending 100% of your monthly rental income!

So, although the concept of a safe-withdrawal rate is flawed as it applies to other investments, including and especially cash, the concept is alive and well when you convert your savings to rental real estate, as I did.

And, even if I left my rentals empty, I would still be making money because, as I write this in late 2013, the real estate market is exploding! AGAIN! I estimate that my properties are appreciating about one percent a month. That means, with an estimated market value of $400,000, I am making $4,000 a month on appreciation alone.

And, remember, that appreciation is compounding! $4,000 in the baseline month, a little more the month after that and the month after that and the month after that...

In the not too distant future, the monthly appreciation amount will hit $5,000 and, if I hold on long enough and the present appreciation rate holds steady or increases, I will hit $6,000 a month.

In other words, I will be making $72,000 a year, if all I do is sit at home watching reality TV shows all day in my underwear!   Not bad for a zero-hour workweek, right? (!!!)

And, because I live in one of the houses I own, I am also enjoying the benefit of imputed income in the amount of, I estimate, $900 a month.

As I have written, after my divorce, I needed my money to work harder, much harder, than it was working by just sitting there in a *guaranteed* account. Now my money is working as hard as I did to earn it!

Cash is king but, when interest rates are low, the king has no clothes. And I invested in rental real estate because that is where the highest and best use of my money was to be had.

CHAPTER TWELVE

I have now (July, 2013) achieved my goal of owning $400,000 worth of real estate. And what that means is that, assuming my assumption about the average increase in house prices is correct, my net worth will grow as follows:

June to June, 2013 – 2014: ($400,000) (1.15) = $460,000

June to June, 2014 – 2015: ($460,000) (1.15) = $529,000

June to June, 2015 – 2016: ($5290,000) (1.15) = $608,000

Again, as far as I am concerned, that appreciation is just like money in the bank, only better! In three years, I plan to sell and retire to writing and living in Mexico full-time. I already split my time between Yuma and Mexico but, little by little, I am spending more and more time at my place on the beach in Baja than in Yuma.

As it is, I now gross over $80,000 a year from my pension, writing, and rental income—a figure that has grown and that I fully expect to grow every year from now on until I cash out my real estate gains!

Add to that amount of my cash income my expected gains from real estate appreciation, and principle reduction on those properties on which I hold a mortgage, and I am making closer and closer to $200,000 a year.

And remember, I don't have a "real" job...although I am earning more now than I ever did back in the days when I used to work for a living!

The first full year since reaching my goal of $400,000 in real estate, my gross will actually be more than $200,000!

How so? Well, as I detailed in my first book, the property I call my *Ranchita* was a foreclosure that was worth, I estimate, $135,000, the day I bought it for $85,000! So, that property—alone—added $50,000 to my bottom-line in 2013

In July of 2013, I bought the property that is my primary residence in Yuma. That property was appraised at the time I purchased it for $120,000. I paid $95,000 for it and so, at the close of escrow, I realized an instant bump in net worth of another $25,000.

If you are keeping track, that is $75,000 of instant net worth on those two properties, alone, at the time of purchase. Add to that figure a year's worth of appreciation, another $60,000, and my $80,000 of income and the total is $205,000!

Again, between the Palm House, the name by which I refer to my personal residence in Yuma, and my ranchita, I banked something like $75,000 in instant equity in 2013!

The Palm House and my *Ranchita* have a combined market value of approximately $255,000 and, to that amount, you can add the value of the house I already owned before my divorce and still own, which has a market value, estimated modestly, by me, to be $125,000.

That brings my total to $380,000, a little short of my goal of $400,000 but, I am hoping, well within the margin of error! That and appreciation might well serve to catch-me-up, if you will.

And, if appreciation in the next couple of years is higher than my assumed rate of 15%, it surely will.

For the sake of banking appreciation (the rise in value of real estate due to inflation, mostly, and other market forces such as supply and demand), it does not matter if you own the property outright or not.

In fact your ROI will almost always be higher if you do have a mortgage. Why? Your ROI will be higher when you finance the property because the appreciated value, which adds to your total ROI, will be computed against a lower figure. For example, you have seen my return of 17.4% on my Palm House.

But, if I had financed that home with just the normal 20% down payment, my gross return would look like this assuming that same 15% annual appreciation rate that is being projected by some experts:

Purchase price: $95,000

Down Payment at 20%: $19,000

Annual Appreciation: ($95,000) (.15) = $14,250

ROI: 14250/19000 = 75% (!!!!)

At that rate my investment would have been doubling every thirteen or fourteen months or so based on appreciation—ALONE!

(I will explain how I arrived at that doubling rate later in the book.)

But, remember, also: The ROI stated above is before taking into account the rental income, tax savings, and imputed income I am realizing as a benefit of living in my house, virtually rent-free! But, remember, too, that that 75% ROI figure represents gross, before the consideration of operating costs.

But, regardless, I expect you are beginning to see how buying and owning as few as one or two rental properties is how you can retire and grow rich.

But buying and holding those same properties for some period of time, exactly how long is determined by your personal financial goals, is how you can retire and grow richer!

CHAPTER THIRTEEN

In my first book, I wrote about the Rule of 72 which states that money doubles at a rate equal to the number 72 divided by your ROI.

And what that means in this particular case is that, when you use leverage to obtain beneficial use of a rental property, which you can readily accomplish by using a mortgage loan to finance your purchase, it is entirely possible to double your money once a year!

Doubling your investment every year, even when you are only talking about $19,000 like we are in the previous example, in and of itself, is pretty impressive, right?

But what if, instead of paying cash to buy my two properties, I had leveraged that money to buy two or three million dollars' worth of rentals? Well, assuming that same 15% appreciation rate, I could be making more like $500,000 a year in appreciation, alone!

And, at that rate, you could cash out in just a couple of years and go live on a beach somewhere!

Now, will that 15% appreciation rate I have assumed in my planning actually hold up over the next three years? Who knows?

It might be less...or, then again, it might be even more!

But all we have to go on is history, right? Well, history and the prognostications of "experts." And the experts are forecasting more than 15% for the coming year in my market!

But, if the experts are correct, I will begin cashing out in late 2015, I plan to sell my *Ranchita* that year. As I already wrote, I purchased that property for some $50,000 under-market.

Three years from the date I purchased it, assuming that 15% annual appreciation rate does indeed pan out, the property should be worth something like $205,000.

Remembering, if you will, that I paid cash for it, I will, in one fell-swoop, as they say, recover just about one-half of all the money I lost in the divorce! Early the following year, I will sell my other two properties and recoup the other $100,000—at least.

And, when I have sold all the real estate I own as I write this, it will be as George Bush said:

Mission Accomplished!

Of course, that was the plan I had on getting back into real estate and, as I write this today, I still plan to stick to it. But who knows, right? By then, I might change my mind and just keep banking the monthly rental income which will, by then, be something like $2,000 a month in cash!

(And do not forget to add my imputed income to that figure—which actually spends just like cash!)

Money in the bank is not my bottom-line, actually, and if I do sell it will be, largely, to divest myself of the risk and responsibility that comes with owning even as few rental properties as I do.

PART THREE

Getting Zen…
And The Some!

CHAPTER FOURTEEN

In this chapter, I will just do a sort of free-style riff about the business of owning rentals, property management, and a little of this and a little of that all related to those subjects...if only barely!

This information is intended as only the barest of primers on the subjects covered and I am assuming that you will research the various topics covered in much greater depth, yourself, before deciding to take the plunge, yourself.

Zen and the Art of Managing Tenants

Managing tenants is part art and part science. The exact mix, however, is pretty much dependent on your own personality. Let me explain this a bit more:

I diversified a part of my retirement income into residential real estate. This is a hybrid business model that is partly a service business but I also own the means of production; that means of production is not my labor but not a machine producing widgets that I sell, either.

When I buy a rental property, it is something like buying a machine that can make money but it is incumbent on me to manage the business in such a way that it does, in fact, operate profitably.

Like any machine, it requires maintenance to continue to operate. And the people who rent my property are like my employees in that they labor to earn the money to pay the rent.

Few property owners think of their tenants as employees or manage them that way. But, in fact, my tenants work for me in a really ideal employer-employee relationship: I do not need to manage them on the job or track their hours or performance; I do not need to pay for their health insurance or contribute to their Social Security or 401k accounts.

My business "sells" housing by the month. It has an inventory but it is, perhaps, the easiest inventory to track and manage of any business other than a business that has no inventory, to speak of, at all.

I do not always enjoy dealing with tenants or the daily aspects of running my business but it pays so well I can't say no.

Each rental "unit," is an individual and independent stream of income that serves to provide me additional income diversification and financial viability. And, each property also provides those six individual streams of income that sort of super-charge those aspects of the business.

Obviously, the single most-important stream of income is that of rent but in addition to that, there is increased net worth achieved when I make the monthly mortgage payment and pay down the balance of the debt thereby increasing my equity.

My net worth also grows as the property appreciates in value; and owning rental property can be a source of tax deductions that can offset taxes on your other income.

If you want to read more about the six streams of rental property income, I cover the subject in more depth in my first book in this series, *Retire and Grow Rich!*.

The management style of managers, regardless of the setting in which that management takes place, tends to fall into one of two camps: Hard-ass or humanitarian.

Hard-ass managers relay more on systems and discipline to get people to do what they want them to do; their management style is more science than art.

Humanitarians, as you have probably guessed by now and as the name implies, display more art in how they manage people. And, the way they manage has to do with the particulars of the situation and the other person involved; their style is also more nuanced and flexible.

I am more of a humanitarian than a hard-ass. Of course, I only have five tenants and I can get away with less science than would probably be the case if had more than that. Of course, the challenge of managing tenants is one reason why I made the conscious decision to keep my rental business small.

Basically, management style depends on whether you think that people will, in general do the right thing, and so do not require constant supervision or you think that, left to their own devices, people will try and get away with whatever they can get away with and so need to be supervised closely to ensure they get the job done.

And, it has also been my experience that the 80/20 Rule applies to managing tenants: 20 percent of your tenants will require 80% of your attention. Ideally, however, you would replace those 20% tenants and eventually have only those tenants that fall into the eighty percent that require less of your attention. Once you are able to accomplish that, you are likely to have few, if any, tenant issues.

Maintaining Your Properties

But, the truth is, even when you have no "problem" tenants, real estate is work, mostly in the form of maintenance. Managing your property will be more about maintaining your properties correctly than it will be about your tenants. And trying to save money by deferring any necessary maintenance is a false economy. And doing so could end up costing you more than doing it when it is required.

In fact, keeping on top of your maintenance schedule can actually save you money. For example, waiting too long to paint the exterior trim on a house could result in the trim needing to be replaced. This will be a much more expensive a proposition that a simple paint job.

Absolute Beginner

It sometimes seems to me as if I make decisions more complicated than they need to be. Some decisions, I know, are hard; especially those that have a lot riding on them. And, really, most of the big decisions, once made, will determine the arc of your life from that point forward.

My decision to divorce my wife, for example, changed my life in almost all aspects. Had I stayed married, my life today would be significantly different. And I would have a higher net worth. And although I plan to recoup my losses in that regard, I am only getting back to square one whereas, if I had made the same investments while remaining married, my net worth would be almost double what it will be by the time I sell out.

You can never really recover lost money, you can only recover lost ground and build from there. But my primary financial goal, for a long time now, has been to be financially independent. I achieved that goal a long time ago but remaining financially independent is now the focus of managing my finances.

At the time of my divorce, and in something of a panic, I worried that I had lost my status as financially independent; that turned out not to be the case. But, even the worry that it might be, made me realize that once you reach a goal, sometimes the goal changes to being that of staying the course.

After I had achieved financial independence, my goal then became to REMAIN financially independent!

And, often, achieving a goal and staying the course will require the implementation of two different strategies.

I never took that consideration into account until forced to do so. But, as I said, I remain financially independent to this day. More money will not make me more financially independent because I do not believe you can qualify the state of being financially independent that way. It is like saying forever and ever…the "ever" is superfluous.

And you are either financially independent or you are not but you can be partially financially independent. What do I mean by that?

Well, I established financial independence as my primary financial goal when I was 33 years old. At the time, I was broke (which I describe as having no savings), unemployed, and almost $50,000 in debt. And I was dependent on family for a place to live!

Not long after that low-point in my life, I found a job. I had made the decision that, when I did find a job, I would save *at least* ten percent of every dollar I earned for the rest of my life; and that is exactly what I started doing and continue doing to this day although, these days, I save much more than ten percent of my earnings.

And as my savings grew, so did the amount of interest I earned every month on those savings. Eventually, as my savings grew and the interest they earned every month likewise grew, I realized that the amount of interest I was earning was equal to about ten percent of my monthly cost of living,

I was, I realized, partially financially independent to the tune of that same ten percent. And, I also realized, that as the amount of interest I was earning grew even more, so would my level of my partial financial independence.

And, although the date would be far in the future, I knew that someday, if I continued to save at my present rate or better, my interest income would be equal to my cost of living and that, at that point, I would be *completely and totally* financially independent!

It was at that point that I made achieving financial independence my primary financial goal. The decision that I would achieve financial independence was the decision that most impacted my financial life from then on...until my decision to divorce.

The decision to get into the real estate business can be, like my decision to get a divorce, a momentous one, as well. But indecision is also a choice, as well.

And a decision will often require you to make yet more decisions.

Decisions, Decisions, Decisions...

But in real estate, the first decision is whether or not to enter the fray. If you decide to go into the business, then you face yet two more and immediate choices:

What kind of properties will you invest in and your investment strategy. In my case, I decided to invest in residential rental properties and my investing protocol is a strategy known as, "buy and hold."

Basically, there are two fundamental real estate investment strategies: One is my approach, buy and hold; the other is what is often referred to as "flipping." Buy and hold (BAH) is just that, you hold on to a property for a long time whereas flipping is acquiring a property with the intention of selling it in the short term.

All else being equal, flipping will require more of an investment and require more expertise. It is also a more intensive process in many ways. I can't tell you a lot about flipping properties as an investment strategy because I have no experience in the field. There is plenty of information out there, however. And it is highly touted as a way to get rich quick via late-night infomercials.

I selected buy-and-hold because I was already familiar with it.

My brother used the strategy to get rich over fifteen years or so. So, I have personally witnessed the BAH strategy produce the intended results. The success of the BAH strategy is dependent, mostly, on the appreciation of property over time; that appreciation, driven, mostly, by nothing more than inflation in the general economy, in general.

And, by the way, that inflation occurs in both the value of the property *and* monthly rents. That may not mean a lot to you now, but it is that appreciation in rents that will help to protect your income from the negative effects of inflation.

Flipping, on the other hand, forces appreciation through improvements in the short-term; properties, usually distressed properties that require repairs, are purchased at a price below what the property would be worth in better condition. The profit is flipping houses comes from repairing the property and then selling it.

When flipping a property, the sooner you are able to get the property ready to sale, and actually sell it, the better because carrying costs will eat into the bottom-line. Every month that goes by, while you are getting the property ready to sell, is another mortgage payment (assuming you have a mortgage), that many more utility bills, and the monthly cost of insurance and taxes are all eating into your profits.

But, again, I know the basics of flipping and the underlying concept is easy enough to grasp, but it is just not my style. Although, like someone looking to do a flip, I also looked for distressed, although only slightly, properties when I was looking to buy.

And, as I said, one of my properties was a foreclosure—can't get much more distressed than that. And when you do buy a property that needs work before it is ready to sell, or in my case to rent, the sooner it is ready to rent, the sooner it will begin producing income. So, buying a distressed property will always have an element of time to it in that regard. Empty properties cost money!

More on the Subject of Imputed Income

I have used the term, "imputed income," several times now throughout the text of this book. It is a sort of nebulous financial concept of sorts having to do with assigning a cash value to value received in some form *other than* cash.

Do you see know what I mean when I say that the concept is *nebulous*?

Even the definition of the term is vague in a way.

So, let me try to explain the concept a different way:

One way rich people get rich is to buy assets that appreciate...that is, that go up in value. One of the most common forms of assets that appreciate is real estate.

Now, I am well aware that the years 2008 through 2011 were tough on real estate prices and that we saw values drop but that was then and this is now!

And now, prices are going up fast! In Phoenix, for example, and as I have already mentioned, prices are up almost 25% from March of last year to March of this year…25%!

The trend in real estate is appreciating values although, yes, sometimes there are periods when prices suffer. But, really, during a down market, you will not feel a thing unless you are forced to sell. And who is least likely to be forced to sell?

The rich, that's who!

The last downturn in the real estate market was driven by a perfect storm of stupid; from banks making it too easy to get mortgages, to historically low interest rates, to buyers buying more than they could actually afford, and just a sort of general financial mania that was in the air at the time.

Real estate appreciation is not free money but there is free money to be had in real estate: Imputed income.

Rent payments and mortgage payments, you see, are not the same thing. Rent payments are what the renter pays for the value of the housing that is received in return for those payments.

Mortgage payments, on the other hand, are what the buyer pays to acquire the asset underlying the mortgage—the house. The buyer pays nothing to live in the house and, so, in effect, lives in the house rent-free.

Those who live in expensive homes not only get to deduct the interest they pay on their mortgage, they also receive a large amount of imputed income, in the form of free rent, every month.

And there is, besides *free* rent, yet another way that the rich benefit from imputed income:

Imputed income is tax-free.

So, they are not only living rent-free, the imputed income they receive in the form of that free rent is tax-free!

In the first year of a one-million dollar mortgage (at 4%), the home-owner will be able to deduct almost $40,000 in mortgage interest.

And, meanwhile, if we assume the $1M figure represents 80% of the purchase price and market-value rent to be one percent of the market value, that same home-owner is receiving imputed income of $12,500 a month!

Adding the two benefits we arrive at a preliminary figure of $190,000…but we are not done yet. Renters pay rent out of their net income.

So, in order to calculate the **net** value of the imputed income being received in the form of free rent, we first need to calculate how much someone would need to earn in order to pay the monthly amount of the rent equal to the imputed income.

If we assume that anyone living in a house valued at $1,250,000 is in the top tax bracket (and this is Federal only!), the real value of the imputed income is almost 40%, that individual would need to gross over $20,000 to net the $12,500 of imputed income he or she is realizing!

The bottom-line, then, in terms of the amount of free money is almost $300,000!

Want to live like the rich?

Buy a house.

Want to get rich?

Buy more than one!

AFTERWORD

AFTERWORD

I accumulated what real estate investing expertise I do possess over the years since I bought my first investment property way back in 1980! I have been in and out of the market ever since buying and selling and restoring properties as my personal investments and residences.

In fact, I have purchased ten properties to live in as my personal residence, at one time or another, and a few of those properties also doubled as rentals since they had more than one unit. That particular investment strategy, alone, made me a lot of money.

When the sh*t hit the fan back in 2010 and my personal life went in the crapper, taking my finances and retirement dreams with them not long after, I turned back to real estate to recover.

Again, I re-entered the real estate fray with two goals:

1. Replace the loss in monthly income that I suffered by way of lost interest on lost retirement savings AND the $700 a month I am obligated to pay my ex until 2017, and;

2. Grow my net worth back to what it was at the time we separated that same year.

As it appears today, as I write this, I have achieved my first goal; in fact, I have exceeded it by a large margin!

As for goal #2, it is now on auto-pilot:

If my properties appreciate at approximately the rate I have assumed, again, based on what the *experts* have projected, I will have recovered my losses about two years from the day I purchased my first investment property.

Barring a global pandemic or a zombie invasion, I expect the US economy to do all the work for me in that regard! I will, just as I have done in the past, sit back and be taken along for a very profitable ride.

As I write these words in the late summer of 2013, the US economy is recovering just as it always has from the cyclical downturn into which we, as a nation, seem to swoon every few years. We are at the dawn of a rising economic tide.

And, as it has been said before, a rising tide lifts all boats...or, it will, if you have a boat on the water. The boat I have launched is that investment vessel with which I am most familiar:

Rental property.

Do not ask me about stocks or bonds or portfolio diversification. Although I am well-read on those and other financial topics, they are not "my thing."

My thing is boots on the ground and getting my hands dirty; I am a blue-collar-type of guy. And I have been since my days as a construction electrician apprentice and, later, a property manager for the US government.

And everything I have accomplished, you can accomplish! In fact, with just a little more ambition, you can not only retire and grow rich, you can, absolutely, retire and grow richer!

Thank for reading!

In the pages that follow is a free preview of
my first book in this series:

Retire and Grow Rich!

APPENDIX ONE

PREVIEW—

Retire and Grow Rich!

RETIRE
AND GROW RICH!

*How I Turned $180,000 of My Retirement
Savings into $11,300,000—in Just 60 Days—
and How You Can, Too!*

Marcus Arce
Meme Media

Retire and Grow Rich!™
Published by Meme Media.

ISBN-13: 978-1484102862
ISBN-10: 148410286X
Copyright © 2013 by Marcus Arce.
All rights reserved.

Printed in the United States of America.

10 9 8 7 6 5 4 3 2 1

This book is dedicated to the 10,000
Baby Boomers that are retiring every day of the
year here in the good ol' US of A...
in particular to those who, like me, came under fire
from the slings and arrows of outrageous fortune at a
time when they could least afford it!

Pray to God but continue rowing to shore.
—Russian proverb

PREFACE

In August of 2012, my marriage of almost ten years ended in divorce. One year before my divorce I had had $600,000 in retirement savings. The day the final decree was signed, one-half of that money was gone.

Between the lawyer fees, the cost of setting up and maintaining a separate household for over a year, support to my wife after our separation, some stupid spending that I engaged in in the hope it would make me feel better, a big loss on the sale of some personal property in Mexico, and the agreed-to divorce settlement, I was out three-hundred grand in less than twelve months.

This was money that I had been counting on to put the shine on my Golden Years. With the stroke of a judge's pen, however, those Golden Years were suddenly looking considerably less glossy!

But in order for you to more fully appreciate the bind that losing that money had put me in, you also need to know that, at the time I divorced, I was sixty years old and had been retired for five years.

And suddenly I was facing the one question that all retirees hope they never have to ask themselves:

Could I afford to stay retired?

Anyone who has ever been through a divorce will know that the process is something like an emotional meat-grinder. And, considering my finances in light of my emotional state at the time, my first reaction was to panic.

My first thought was that I had to find a job fast to stop the bleeding! But my second thought was to consider the harsh reality that finding a job at my age, after five years out of the job market, was going to be tough and my options limited.

If finding a job was Plan A, then, what I needed, I quickly realized, was a Plan B. This book is the story of the Plan B I came up with—and how putting that plan into action saved my retirement!

Table of Contents

PREFACE
Page VII

INTRODUCTION
Page XI

INTRODUCTION

I have been investing in real estate since 1980 but I am no expert on the subject. So, I am sure you must be wondering, "Where does this guy get off writing a book on real estate if he's no expert on the subject?"

Well, as I see it, writing a book on any given subject is like investing in real estate—if you wait until all concerned can agree that you are, in fact, an expert, the book will never get written—and the money just waiting to made will remain just another pipe dream...

But I am an expert on what worked for me! And that is what this book is about—it is *my* story. Your results, however and of course, may vary...as they say...whoever "they" are!

And here is what I think I know based on my own experiences—what worked for me can, absolutely, work for you. How do I know that with such certainty? Because what worked for me was what I knew for a fact had worked for others including some in my own family!

And all I did to achieve the success I have had in real estate was to copy a few known investing strategies with a few wrinkles of my own added to the mix to accomplish the specific goals *I* had in mind.

There is a known and proven strategy to achieve success in real estate investing. The strategy is simple: buy as much property as you need to in order to achieve your goals.

For most of us who invest in real estate for the income it provides, that GOAL will be a certain amount of monthly income. In my case, my primary goal was to create an extra $2,000 a month in NET income.

And here is the good news:

There is nothing in particular that is so tricky or difficult or challenging about investing in real estate or managing a few rental properties that you can't learn or successfully apply yourself...just like those same real estate strategies have been learned and applied by countless others before you, including myself.

If you are in the target market for this book, that is, if you are a retired person who wants or needs to generate some additional monthly income, it is likely that you have a wealth of life experience to draw on and that the skills and abilities YOU ALREADY POSSESS will pave the way for success in your real estate venture.

You already know simple math and possess certain people skills, you probably have something of a discerning real estate eye and know a little about your local community.

Well, guess what? Those are pretty much what and all it takes to begin—it is the actual beginning, the hurdle of actually *doing* something with the information you are about to read, that is usually the hardest part!

And, please, be forewarned, if you are reading this part of the book as part of a preview on Amazon or on my webpage, this is not the only real estate book you will need to read to become more familiar with the topic.

This book is intended to be a nothing more than an introduction to the subject of real estate investing.

And, to that disclaimer, I will add one more, still:

This is not a book about real estate investing in the traditional sense.

Instead, in this book, I will share with you my personal story of how just a couple real estate investments enabled me to remain retired when the financial rug was pulled out from under me.

This book is intended to relate to you how I did that and serve as something of a primer on the broader subject of real estate investing, in general.

In the pages that follow, I will give you the foundation of knowledge you will need to understand *why and how* real estate will work to help my target audience achieve the extra income they desire.

But the single most important lesson of this book is that you are also going to learn the driving force that propels real estate investing profits.

Many people don't know that, you know? Do you? Do you know how real estate has created more millionaires than any other form of investment?

You see, most of us have heard of people making money in real estate, but have no idea where, exactly, those profits come from. In this book you will learn exactly *how and why* a few real estate rentals could be your ticket to more money in retirement—just like they have been for me!

After I retired in late-2007, I found myself with a lot of time on my hands. I did not realize how much time it took to work for a living and when I reclaimed all that time for myself, I started fighting boredom and watching too much TV.

In fact, surveys have revealed that time spent (wasted?) watching TV goes up by an average of 70% after a person retires! I have a Kindle short, *Retirement Regrets* that, previously, was only available for download but that I included in this book for free in Appendix One.

In *Retirement Regrets*, I go into greater details about why I think TV viewing jumps like that among retirees. For the time being, suffice it to say that my real estate investments not only provided me with enough additional income to stay retired but they also keep me about as busy and *engaged* as I want to be, actually!

And, by providing me both extra income and meaningful work, real estate turned out to be a Godsend for me.

And, finally, I will recommend the next few books you should read to get your feet wet, if you are a relative or absolute novice in the field, as all we more-seasoned investors once were. You are in the exact position all of us who are making money in real estate today once stood.

Investing in real estate, a rental property, in particular, can provide you with additional monthly income in the form of extra cash in your pocket but it can also provide you with, what is known as, *imputed income*, which I will get into later.

But as important as both those types of income are, the real benefit of diversifying a portion of your retirement savings into real estate is that doing so has been historically proven to help fight the effects of inflation on those saving.

So, just to be clear and so that you understand exactly what is in this book:

You will read my story and see the exact and actual numbers that show how much more I earn every month with my real estate investments than I was earning on that same amount of money in *secure* cash investments.

And you will learn how real estate works to produce those returns and how that same dynamic will help you beat the **Number One** financial enemy that every retired person must face and that will, from the day you retire, threaten your hopes to remain retired!

PART ONE

Remembering Games

Chapter One

Let's begin, then, with the actual numbers:

The purchase price of my two investment properties, which included four houses and two trailers, was $95,000 for one and $85,000 for the other for a total of $180,000 of my $300,000 in retirement savings being invested.

That $180,000 had been earning an average of .003% of annual interest—in other words, less than $600 a year. Here is the exact math:

180,000 x .003 = $540/year

After I had purchased the two properties, moved into one of the houses and rented the other three houses and one of the trailers, here is what I was earning on a monthly basis:

Property One:

House One: $900 (this is where I presently reside; this amount is *imputed income*, which I will explain, shortly…)

House Two: $550 (Rent/Cash)

Total of Monthly Income Property One: $1,450

Property Two:

House One: $775
House Two: $425
Trailer One: $175

Total of Monthly Rents Property Two: $1,375

$1,375 + 550 + 900 (Imputed Income) = $2,825/per Month or $33,900/per Year!

33,900/180000 = >18.8%

18.8/.003 = >6,266 times as much!

But the real and eye-opening question we need to ask is this:

How much would my retirement savings need to be to earn that same $2,825 every month if they were invested at the same .003% return that I had been earning on them?

Well, to answer that question, let's figure out how much a million dollars would earn every year at that same .003% interest rate:

$1,000,000/.003 = $3,000

OK...let's do the math:

A million dollars earning .003% would earn you $3,000 a year. My real estate rentals and the imputed income from my personal residence were making me over eleven times that amount:

33,900/3000 = 11.3

11.3 x $1,000,000 = $11,300,000!

11,300,000/33,900 = .003.

So, in order to earn the $33,900 I was earning as rental and imputed income, at the average interest rate I was getting from the banks at the time, I would have needed to have had over $11,000,000 in the bank! And, hence, the subtitle of this book:

How I Turned $180,000 in Retirement Savings into $11,300,000—in 60 Days...

I am certain that when you first read that, you were certain that is was simply hyperbole intended to sell books, right? Well, now you know the truth!

And, actually, the actual return I am realizing these days is much, much higher, as you will learn later in the book.

Also, you will learn why, I don't care if real estate values go down; in fact, one of the best times to own rental properties is when the economy is bad.

Why? Because when times get tough, more people rent. And, when more people rent, rents go up!

And, when the economy is good, guess what? It is also one of the best times to own rental properties!

How can that be? Because when times are good, the rate of inflation will usually increase and rents tend to follow the same trajectory as a rise in the inflation rate.

In other words, good times or bad, rents always go up!

Chapter Two

I am a very conservative investor and my retirement savings were "invested" entirely in interest-bearing cash accounts and, at that time in late-2012, those savings were earning an average return of 0.003%.

That's right—about one-third of one percent! And the rates had been stuck at historically low rates for a couple of years by then—but what was worse about that whole scenario is that those rates were not going to go up for the foreseeable future!

In actual cash, the $300,000 I had left after my divorce, was earning me less than a measly fifty bucks a month in interest! In order to be able to afford to stay retired I would need more income—a lot, lot more than $50 a month, that was for sure!

And I needed it fast as every day that passed was eroding the real worth of that money even further. I knew of only a single investment opportunity, other than cash, with which, the idea of which, I was comfortable, real estate—residential rental properties, to be exact.

This, then, is the story of how I turned an amount of money that had been earning me less than fifty bucks a month—before taxes!—into a handful of appreciating assets and income of almost $34,000 a year—over 60 times as much!

An amount that actually made the difference between staying retired or being faced with the daunting task of having to find a job at my age—which I knew would be almost impossible, regardless!

By the way—*and this is a very important aside here*—that three-hundred grand that I had sitting in the bank was actually a depreciating asset because the annual rate of inflation was actually greater than the average of the returns I was earning on those savings.

In other words, without ever spending a dime of that money, the actual value of those savings was less every day—day after day!

So the clock was ticking. The spending power my savings represented was going downhill fast and gaining momentum.

I was fighting a losing battle to preserve the value of the money I had worked so hard and so long to save—what I had left of it, that is! I did not have the luxury of time—I needed to do something to arrest the free fall and I needed it fast!

To tell you the truth, I felt pretty terrible at the time and not a little desperate out of concern for my finances!

So, let's recap my situation at the time:

Half my money gone up in smoke, divorced, schlepping my dirty clothes to the local Laundromat in a fifteen year-old car (bought off a street-corner the day before I had to turn my car over to my ex as part of the settlement), and, to top it all off, my damn plantar fasciitis was killing me...

But things were about to take a turn for the better!

And, as it turned out, in less than two months—the fabled sixty days of the subtitle of this book—I had—almost as if by magic...or was it alchemy?—turned $50 a month into more than $2,800 a month!

Chapter Three

It was October, 2012. My divorce was not yet two months old and a friend was letting me stay in a small, one-bedroom house he owned in the nearby town of San Luis Rio Colorado, Sonora, Mexico.

I was, basically, hiding out there while trying to find a more permanent living arrangement north of the border, having lost the home my ex-wife and I had lived in together before the divorce to her in the divorce as part of the final decree.

So, like the cherry topping an ice cream sundae, I was, basically, homeless, if not without resources and a lifetime of experience to draw on.

Not that I looked at in in quite that positive a light at the time! At the time, I felt like I was adrift in a small boat on a large, dark sea with even darker clouds gathering overhead. And, for the first time in my life, I had no place to call home.

I spent those days taking long walks alone, thinking, getting pissed off at my ex-wife, and walking some more, thinking some more, getting even more pissed off at my ex-wife, and looking for a piece of real estate to buy that might pull my ass out of the financial fire—namely two to four units on a single lot.

I needed that sort of property, that is, a duplex or fourplex, in particular, because I was hoping that the rents I received from the unit or units I was not living in would be sufficient to pay the mortgage and thereby allow me to live, essentially, rent-free.

If I could swing that sort of living arrangement, I could recoup the support I was providing my ex as required by the terms of our divorce settlement. And, by doing that, I was hoping I would realize the same pre-divorce, net monthly income.

That day in October, I was in the middle of my scouting when I passed a property with a for-sale posted in the front yard. I parked the car and took note that the property was empty. I stood on the lawn and peered over the fence at the various structures on the lot. "This could work," I thought.

Then I took note of the address and contact number from the for-sale sign, got back in my clunker, and drove directly to the nearby public library to research the listing on the internet.

That trip to the library was necessary, by the way, because I had no internet access in the house in Mexico where I was living at the time; that and the fact that I had lost my (*our?*) computer in the divorce.

There, at the library, using a public computer and the free internet access the library provided, I found the property on the website, realtor.com. It was a larger home, a smaller home, and two mobile homes…trailers. The asking price was $95,000 and it was a foreclosure.

I called the listing agent and asked him to write an offer of $78,000 for the property, telling him that I would go to his office to sign the offer so he could submit it ASAP.

Again, this was late 2012 and the real estate market was coming out of the doldrums it had been in for the past five years. Investors were flooding back into the market and snapping up the good deals like the proverbial hotcakes!

And the property in question did look like a good deal to me…so I knew I would have to move fast.

The agent told me he could have the offer ready in about twenty minutes. I jumped back into my car and drove straight to the agent's office and signed the offer.

This was before I had even seen the inside of the properties although the offer included a fourteen-day inspection period contingency that would allow me to withdraw my offer if the results of that inspection were unacceptable to me.

Two days later, the agent informed me that the offer had been rejected. The good news was that no other offers had been received in the meantime. I raised my offer to $85,000 and the agent submitted it; the next day I was informed that the offer had been accepted.

Using a part of my retirement savings, I paid cash and escrow was scheduled to close in three weeks.

One week later, it was November now, another real estate agent I knew called me in regards to a new listing that had just come on the market. Although I was already in escrow for the other property, I agreed to meet him at the property to take a look.

This second property also met my criteria. It was a smaller house of almost 1,000 square feet and a larger house of almost 2,000 square feet. The two houses were situated on a large, commercial lot of almost one acre in size.

The asking price for that property was $109,000. After an inspection that revealed some needed repairs, I made an offer of $95,000 and it was accepted.

So, using yet another chunk of my remaining retirement savings, I also paid cash for that property.

In less than ten days I had acquired two properties that included four houses, two trailers, a commercial acre, and an acre and one-half, in-town ranchita zoned for horses—a place I have affectionately taken to calling my *Ranchita…*

Based on my own knowledge of the rental market in Yuma, I knew that, once all my properties were rented, I could expect to *gross* approximately $2,800 a month in rental income.

And, also based on my past real estate experience, that I would *net* that $2,000 a month I had set as the goal of my investing.

As I wrote previously, from the depths of despair, a light shone and things were looking up! I would not have to become a Walmart Greeter, after all! (not that there's anything wrong with that…)

Now, I just had to decide which of the units I would live in myself, move-in, get the other places rented, and find a girlfriend!

Chapter Four

If you are new to the concept and practice of investing in residential rental properties as a means of generating additional monthly income, you first need to know what drives real estate profits.

You see, it is only when you understand where the money comes from, that is, that you know exactly how real estate *works*, that you will you ever have the confidence to invest your precious retirement savings.

And here is the bottom-line in that regard: Real estate profits are generated by not one but several market forces, the primary among them being inflation.

And, actually, it is not *just* inflation that most empowers real estate profits but, rather, *compounded inflation*—the fact that inflation, itself, *inflates* the effect of inflation to raise prices over time!

The price of everything just keeps going up, right? I mean, that prices go up is a fact as inexorable as the march of time.

And it does NOT matter to my investment strategy if the price increase is somewhat illusory when adjusted for inflation; in absolute dollars, stuff is going to cost more this time next year and even more the year after that.

I remember, when I was a kid, paying a nickel for a bottle of Coke from one of those ubiquitous bright-red vending machines. A *bottle* of Coke, made of plastic now, will cost over twenty times that much now! That price increase? That is the effect (mostly) of inflation in the economy!

Now, if we were talking about the price of a candy bar at Walmart, you might not feel the pinch of inflation….no big deal, right?

No big deal, right. But price inflation when the baseline is minimal, like that candy bar, is still like a frog in a pan of water on the stove who doesn't notice when the flame is turned on and that the water is getting hotter and hotter.

Eventually that frog will get his ass cooked!

Small price increases, like small temperature increases, can cook your retirement plans. When you retire, you need a plan to fight inflation every bit as much as that frog needs to exit that pan—and the sooner that plan is in place the better!

And real estate can be that plan simply because it puts inflation to work in your favor! Inflation will act to raise the price of real estate just like it will raise the price of everything else! And better still, it will raise the amount of rent you can charge as time goes by, as well.

That is pretty much the bottom-line and here it is stated for you in black and white:

When it comes to real estate and inflation in the real estate market, it is what has made a lot of people very rich.

And inflation is also the single dynamic of real estate investing that can and that *will* provide you with extra cash every month, protect the value of your capital, and grow your net worth!

Yea, yea, yea…I know…as I write this in early 2013 we are coming out of a period of time when real estate prices crashed and then continued to slide for like another three years. But also as I write this, the market is recovering and prices are beginning to revert to the more historical trend line…that trend line being up.

In fact, in Phoenix, Arizona, according to some reports, prices are up 25% since last year! Why do I mention Phoenix, in particular? Because I live in Arizona.

In Yuma, where I live, real estate prices, by some estimates, are up 17% in that same time-frame. If that is true and the trend holds, I will be making an extra, tax-free $2,000 maybe $3,000 a month—or more!—in appreciation!

Chapter Five

My brother, Jim, was one of those who got rich by investing in residential real estate.

Over the course of twenty years I would visit my brother and, inevitably, the talk would turn to the real estate market. Sometimes the market was good and sometimes it was bad. Always the prices were higher than the last time we had talked.

"Jim," I would say, "there is no way prices can go any higher." Certain I was right because I had a graduate degree in business and another degree in California Real Estate Practices and Jim never made it out of the eighth grade. Certain I was right because I was an executive in the Federal Government and he was a barber.

Jim would reply, "Buy now, prices are going up." And who was always right? You know, right? We here today all have the luxury of hindsight. And we all know that hindsight is twenty-twenty but how did Jim know—back then?

Where did his vision come from? Based on what education? Where did that faith come from and what was the foundation of that faith?

In every instance after that conversation, I would ask myself those questions as I drove away. Knowing that this time he would be wrong and I would be right. I was never right and he was never wrong.

And even coming out of a period of declining real estate values, a period that some have termed, The Great Recession, still Jim is being proven right...almost ten years after he passed away. Leaving an estate, I might add, of several million dollars!

What I failed to realize at that time was that my brother, Jim, was a great American and that a large part of his faith in the system was based on his belief in the American Dream.

He had over forty years of experience to draw on and he had watched the US go into hard times and come back stronger than ever: Time after time after time. America had never failed him in this regard!

The tide would wax and wane: That's what tides do. But when the tide went up, he knew that it would raise all the boats on the water.

And he also realized that in order to take advantage of the power of the tide to lift all boats, you had to be on the water.

An ancient philosopher said that no ship favors a boat without a destination—Jim knew exactly where he was headed!

Jim didn't have a graduate degree or my years of formal education but, on the other hand, I didn't have his degree of certainty in the power of the US economy. And his degree trumped my degree!

Jim was a millionaire at forty. Jim was a multi-millionaire at forty-five. At any time he could have taken his winnings off the table and I often wondered why he didn't. Now I realize that to do so would have meant that he had lost his faith…but he never did.

Jim kept his boat on the water. And he kept taking chances; kept buying properties.

He could have even pulled back, played it safe; kept his boat at anchor in the safety of the harbor of what he had already accomplished. But Jim knew that that is not what boats are for: If you don't want to venture into deep water, you buy a pier not a boat.

And rental properties, residential rental properties, are the perfect investment vehicle for retirement savings for a bunch of reasons besides and in addition to the fact that both the value of the property and the rent you receive will both keep up with inflation….

…as if those two reasons alone are not a sufficient reason alone to invest your retirement savings in real estate!

If you are planning to retire, let me give you a word of advice based on my own experience—don't! I mean, feel free leave the rat race of nine-to-five if you are in the blessed position to do so, but make sure you have something to fill all that time.

I retired without that plan and had way, way too much idle time on my hands. I thought I would love being retired, and I did, for a while.

But, then, I started to get bored. My rental property investments not only saved my retirement, they saved my sanity. These days I can work as much or as little as I feel like on any given day. I always have a project or two on the back-burner that I can have at when I feel like doing so.

Or I can stop by and visit one tenant or another to see how things are going and to check that the property is being cared for. And twice a year I have a BBQ for my tenants as a way to say thank you. After all, it is their rent checks that keep me retired!

PART TWO

How Real Estate Fortunes Are Made 101

This Concludes the Preview

To Read More Go to Amazon.Com

And, again, thank you for reading…

and best of luck!

www.ingramcontent.com/pod-product-compliance
Lightning Source LLC
Chambersburg PA
CBHW051318170526
45166CB00002B/598